AMAZING ARTWORKS

THE WORLD'S BIGGEST, OLDEST, MOST JAW-DROPPING CREATIONS

ÉVA BENSARD • CHARLOTTE MOLAS

T tra.publishing

THE VERY FIRST...

What are the oldest artworks we know of?
When and where did they appear?
Find out on this very first page!

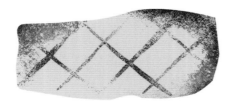

73,000 YEARS AGO
First drawing
Blombos Cave, South Africa
These are crosshatched marks made on a fragment of rock.
Homo sapiens could already handle a "pencil" before
migrating to Europe.

73,000 YEARS AGO
First jewelry
Blombos Cave, South Africa
Our distant ancestors already
appreciated jewelry. The first
necklaces and bracelets were made
from pierced shells.

40,000 YEARS AGO
First stencil
Borneo, Southeast Asia
The first inhabitants of this Indonesian island left
images of their hands on the walls of a cave.

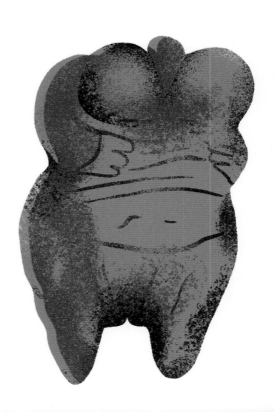

40,000–35,000 YEARS AGO
First human statuette
The Venus of Hohle Fels, **Germany**
This is the oldest prehistoric Venus figure. Discovered
in a cave in 2008, it is tiny (just over 2 inches tall) and
weighs just over 1 ounce! This curvaceous female
statuette was sculpted out of ivory
from a mammoth tusk.

21,000 YEARS AGO
First face
The Lady with the Hood or
Venus of Brassempouy, **France**
A minuscule masterpiece, as tall as three grains of rice!

AROUND 35,000 YEARS AGO
First large animal paintings
Chauvet Cave, France
This is not the first time that humans painted animals, because an even older scene was found in Indonesia. Chauvet is exceptional because of the number of its images (more than 400 paintings and carvings) and their quality.

The first art supplies
Prehistoric artists went shopping in a giant supermarket: nature!
Here's what they could find:
• Ocher: this red or yellow-brown rock can be used as a colored pencil or for painting
• Charcoal, which makes a great black pencil
• Animal hair for brushes
• Flint points for carving

18,000 YEARS AGO
First pottery
Xianrendong, China
The oldest fragments of pottery were discovered in a cave in China. These first clay pots were used to preserve and cook food.

THE OLDEST MASTERPIECES OF HUMANITY

Long before the Lascaux cave, prehistoric people had already created wonders! The proof lies in these two 35,000-year-old art collections: the Chauvet cave paintings (France) and small statuettes found in the Swabian Jura (Germany).

THE CHAUVET CAVE PAINTINGS

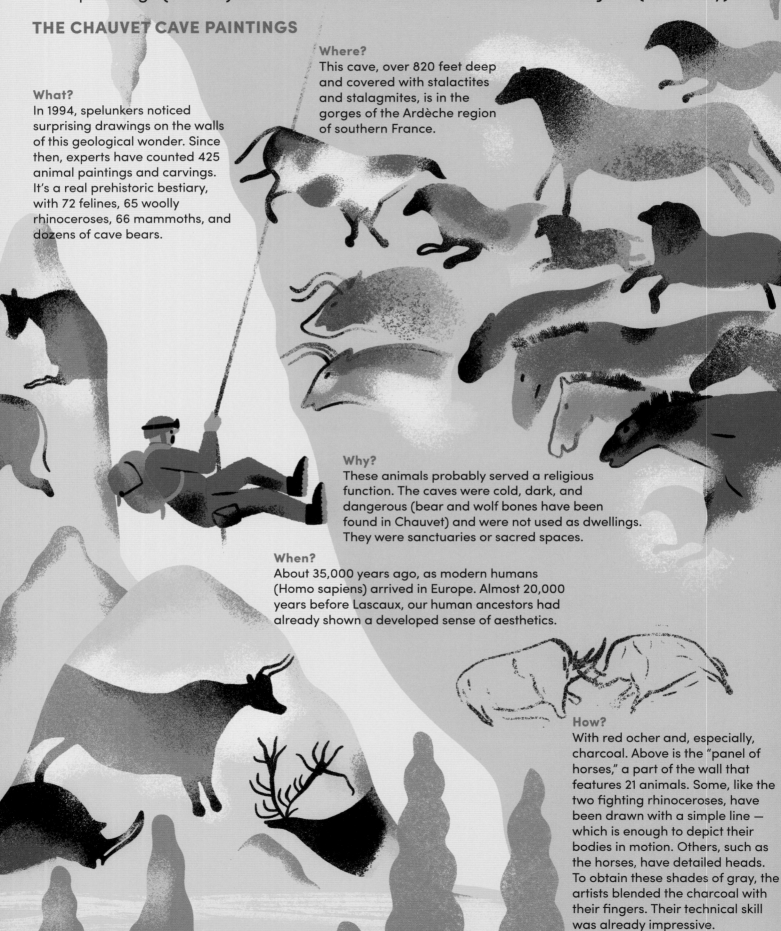

What?
In 1994, spelunkers noticed surprising drawings on the walls of this geological wonder. Since then, experts have counted 425 animal paintings and carvings. It's a real prehistoric bestiary, with 72 felines, 65 woolly rhinoceroses, 66 mammoths, and dozens of cave bears.

Where?
This cave, over 820 feet deep and covered with stalactites and stalagmites, is in the gorges of the Ardèche region of southern France.

Why?
These animals probably served a religious function. The caves were cold, dark, and dangerous (bear and wolf bones have been found in Chauvet) and were not used as dwellings. They were sanctuaries or sacred spaces.

When?
About 35,000 years ago, as modern humans (Homo sapiens) arrived in Europe. Almost 20,000 years before Lascaux, our human ancestors had already shown a developed sense of aesthetics.

How?
With red ocher and, especially, charcoal. Above is the "panel of horses," a part of the wall that features 21 animals. Some, like the two fighting rhinoceroses, have been drawn with a simple line — which is enough to depict their bodies in motion. Others, such as the horses, have detailed heads. To obtain these shades of gray, the artists blended the charcoal with their fingers. Their technical skill was already impressive.

THE STATUETTES OF THE SWABIAN JURA

Where?
In Hohle Fels, Geißenklösterle, Vogelherd, and Hohlenstein-Stadel: four small caves in the Swabian Jura, a mountainous region in southwestern Germany.

What?
About 20 miniature sculptures: mammoths, felines, bears, rhinoceroses...exactly the same species as at Chauvet! Some statuettes were found broken into pieces, including "the lion-man," the biggest of the collection (11 inches tall). Researchers had to reassemble over 300 ivory fragments to put it back together. This prehistoric puzzle took years of work.

When?
About 35,000 years ago, like Chauvet.

Why?
These statuettes may have been amulets or protective objects: their surface is worn, which implies they were used a great deal.

How?
Using durable tools, the artists cut and then sculpted mammoth tusks. Ivory is a hard material that is difficult to sculpt, and yet we see such detailed craftsmanship! The animals are perfectly recognizable, even though they are only a few inches in size. Some of the most refined ones are a small horse and a duck in mid-flight—the first bird figure in the history of humanity.

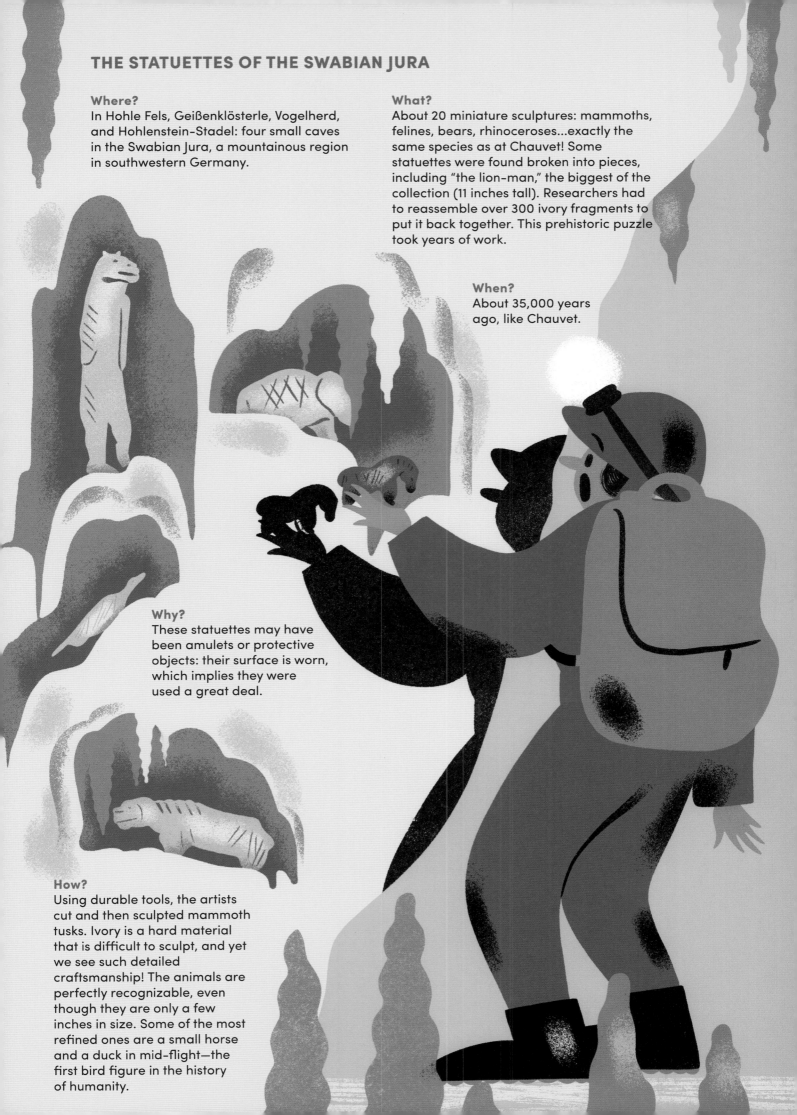

THE GREATEST ARCHAEOLOGICAL DISCOVERIES

Like detectives of the past, archaeologists dig underground searching for traces and clues. Sometimes, they find treasure! Here are five of their most incredible discoveries.

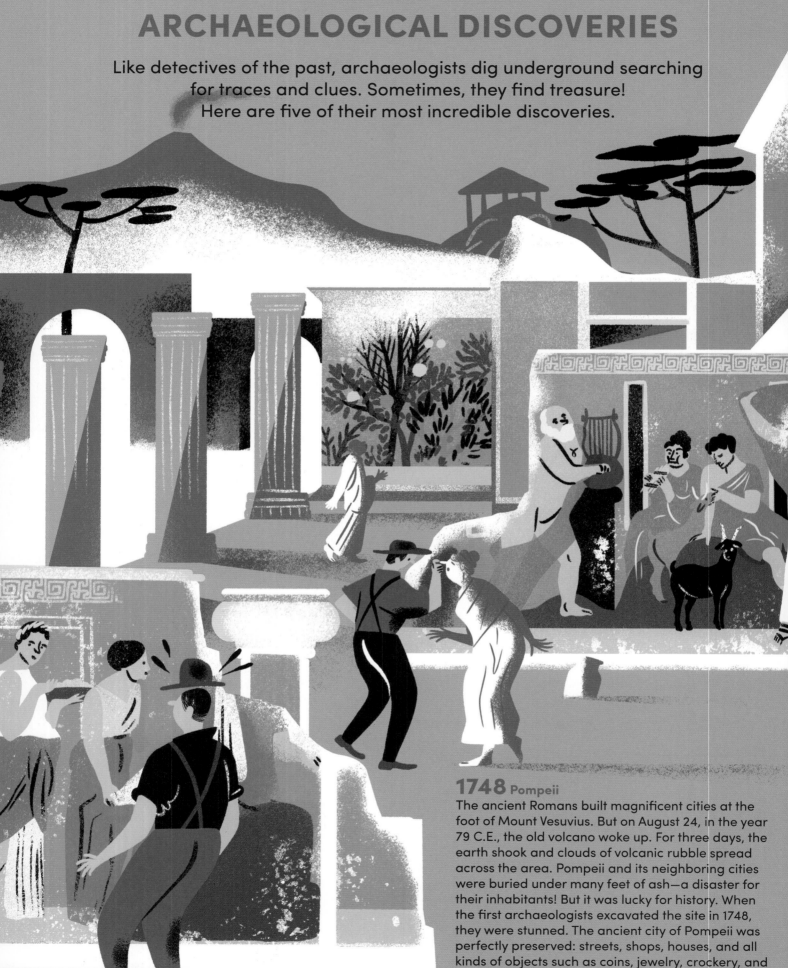

1748 Pompeii

The ancient Romans built magnificent cities at the foot of Mount Vesuvius. But on August 24, in the year 79 C.E., the old volcano woke up. For three days, the earth shook and clouds of volcanic rubble spread across the area. Pompeii and its neighboring cities were buried under many feet of ash—a disaster for their inhabitants! But it was lucky for history. When the first archaeologists excavated the site in 1748, they were stunned. The ancient city of Pompeii was perfectly preserved: streets, shops, houses, and all kinds of objects such as coins, jewelry, crockery, and tools. Pompeii was an infinite trove of discoveries and helped to reconstruct the daily life of the ancient Romans in detail.

1922 Tutankhamun's tomb

Had the Valley of the Kings, where Egypt's pharaohs are buried, revealed all its secrets? Egyptologist Howard Carter was convinced it hadn't. For years, the young man conducted ceaseless digs. Nothing stopped him—not the blazing sun, not even cobra attacks. In November 1922, one step, then two, then three were revealed beneath the sand...the staircase led to a room filled with 2,000 objects! And this was only the beginning. It took Carter ten years to study the entire tomb and inventory its 5,398 treasures. The most fabulous was King Tut's massive gold sarcophagus, which contained his mummy and his death mask.

1974 The mausoleum of the first emperor of China

On March 29, 1974, while digging to build a well, farmers in northern China struck a clay statue as big as a person. Archaeologists then excavated thousands more statues of soldiers, chariots pulled by horses, and horsemen—all very well preserved even though they were 2,200 years old. This terra cotta army protected the gigantic tomb of Qin Shi Huang, China's first emperor. He employed 700,000 workers to build his mausoleum. Only the edges of the structure have been excavated. Who knows what other wonders it may still hold?

1911 Machu Picchu

Imagine a city built on a rocky peak of the Andes range at an altitude of almost 8,000 feet. A true architectural marvel, this 15th-century Inca citadel gradually fell into oblivion. Until July 24, 1911, when, after a long hike through untouched rain forest, American explorer Hiram Bingham found himself face to face with majestic ruins. The site of Machu Picchu ("old mountain" in Quechua) became famous all over the world, and Bingham became legendary. He later inspired Steven Spielberg to create another mythic figure: Indiana Jones.

1922 The royal tombs of Ur

1922 was a good year for archaeology. Another English archaeologist, Leonard Woolley, made a wonderful discovery in Iraq. He uncovered tombs from the ancient city of Ur, one of the most important cities of the ancient Middle East. The tombs contained statuettes, gold diadems, royal musical instruments, and much more. One of the most exceptional pieces is the Standard of Ur, a 4,500-year-old chest with mosaics that transport us to the midst of battles and royal banquets of this period.

GIANT STATUES

It has taken a wealth of patience and ingenuity to build colossal statues that display political, economic, or religious power. Here's an overview of these giants of stone, wood, metal, or concrete.

> 230 feet
The Leshan Giant Buddha, 8th century C.E.
Carved into the rock of a Chinese mountain, this peaceful stone giant is said to have been sculpted by a Buddhist monk in order to calm the rough waters of the river. Everything about this Buddha is gigantic: his shoulders (92 feet wide), his feet (26 feet long), his ears (23 feet), and even his toenails, which are each the size of a person!

> 17 feet
David **by Michelangelo, 1504**
In Florence, Italy, the cradle of the Renaissance, Michelangelo was the first to conquer a block of marble this big. The statue depicts the biblical hero David ready to challenge the giant Goliath. This sculpture has become the symbol of the city of Florence.

> 65 feet
The Great Sphinx of Giza, around 2,500 B.C.E.
It's as tall as a building and as long as a soccer field. The Egyptian artists who achieved this amazing feat also built pyramids and other colossal statues. For over 4,500 years, this "lion-king" has watched over the pyramids of Giza, near Cairo.

> 98 feet
Christ the Redeemer of Rio, 1931
Perched on the Corcovado mountain, it overlooks Guanabara Bay in Rio de Janeiro, Brazil. A structure of reinforced concrete holds it up. This statue was designed by French sculptor Paul Landowski, an artist who specialized in oversized monuments.

> 37 feet
Totem pole of Haida Gwaii, 1882
Native Americans had a custom of erecting these poles of sculpted wood in front of their houses. The stacked figures of bears, ravens, wolves, and eagles represent the ancestors of each family or clan.

> 300 feet
The Statue of Liberty, 1886
This iconic New York statue was made in France. Its metal frame was constructed by the engineer Gustave Eiffel (builder of the Eiffel Tower), while its "ancient" look was designed by sculptor Auguste Bartholdi. A gift from France to the United States, it crossed the Atlantic Ocean by ship.

> 650 feet
The Statue of Unity, 2018
This is the tallest statue in the world: 790 feet including its base! This bronze colossus represents one of the fathers of Indian independence, Vallabhbhai Patel.
Visitors will soon be able to go inside, where a hotel and museum will be built.
This massive project has ruffled a few feathers in India due to its nationalistic over-tones and exorbitant cost.

THE GREAT WALL OF CHINA, THE LONGEST MONUMENT

4,380 mi

M

3,140 mi

Like a giant dragon, the Great Wall winds along ridges and continues its wild ride through valleys and mountains. It climbs to an altitude of over 3,900 feet and rolls through thousands of miles from East to West. It was built to protect the northern border of the Chinese empire. It took over 2,000 years to construct, between the 5th century B.C.E. and the 17th century C.E.

It's the longest monument in the world. Exactly how long is it? It's hard to say, for some sections have been destroyed or turned into villages or roads. But we know that the best-preserved part, built under the Ming dynasty (1368–1644), is almost 5,000 miles long. That's farther than the distance from New York City to Paris!

3,760 mi

💬 **Notable quote:**
"He who hasn't climbed the Great Wall is not a brave man." (Mao Zedong, leader of the People's Republic of China from 1949 to 1976)

The Great Wall by the numbers
13,171 mi estimated total length
5,500 mi preserved today
Between **16 and 23 feet** wide
Up to **56 feet** tall
16 million visitors per year

THE VERY FIRST...

From ancient times to the Renaissance, a series of advances and inventions transformed ways of drawing, painting, and sculpting.

5TH CENTURY B.C.E.
First still lifes in Greece
Greek painters were masters of illusion. They say that Zeuxis painted bunches of grapes that were so realistic that birds tried to peck at them!

AROUND 500 B.C.E.
First large sculptures in West Africa
"Nok" sculptures
These terracotta figures up to 10 feet tall are the oldest sculptures found in sub-Saharan Africa.

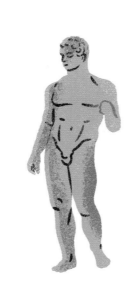

AROUND 440 B.C.E.
First realistic male nude in Greece
The Doryphoros
For the ancient Greeks, these were the proportions of the perfect man. This sculpture by Polykleitos would influence all of Western art history.

AROUND 360 B.C.E.
First realistic female nude in Greece
The Aphrodite of Knidos
For the first time, an artist —Praxiteles— dared to sculpt a nude goddess and show the beauty of her body.

1ST CENTURY C.E.
First personal portraits in Egypt
The Fayum mummy portraits
These fascinating paintings with their large, expressive eyes were placed on Egyptian mummies during the Roman era. They depicted the faces of the deceased.

AROUND 1100
First icons in Russia
Virgin of Vladimir
This is one of the oldest and most venerated Russian icons. The greatest Russian painters were tasked with producing these holy images.

4TH CENTURY C.E.
First "superstar" landscapes in China
The Egyptians, the Greeks, and the Romans had already painted landscapes to decorate their houses or graves. Another vision of landscapes appeared in China. It was no longer just a setting, but the main subject of the painting.

EARLY 15TH CENTURY
First oil paintings in Flanders
The Van Eyck brothers were among the first to master this technique. The colors were no longer mixed with egg, but with oil. This resulted in brilliant hues.

1427
First painting with linear perspective in Italy
Masaccio, *Holy Trinity*
The architecture surrounding this crucifixion seems to be three-dimensional: Masaccio created the illusion of depth although he painted this image on a flat wall. This feat inspired Renaissance artists.

CHILD PRODIGIES IN ART

$$\frac{3+4i}{6}z + \frac{5-}{6}z = z$$
$$(3+4i)(x+iy) +$$
$$(8x - 4y) + i(4x$$

Albrecht Dürer (1471–1528)

His father, who was a goldsmith, taught him drawing and engraving. But the boy's talent quickly surpassed that of his father. At age 13, he made an impressively detailed self-portrait by looking in a mirror. At 15, he learned to paint. He then revolutionized art a few years later, introducing new discoveries from the Italian Renaissance into German art.

Leonardo da Vinci (1452–1519)

From childhood, he was gifted in everything. He could solve complicated math problems, sculpt clay, draw building plans, sing like a bird, and play like a virtuoso. At age 20, he painted his first masterpiece: the figure of the angel in *The Annunciation*, a painting by his teacher Verrocchio. They say that the painter was so dismayed to see his student surpass him that he never picked up a brush again.

Velázquez (1599–1660)

Little Diego handled a brush so well that at age 10, he was apprenticed to a painter in Seville (his hometown) and learned how to grind pigments and stretch canvases. At the time, children learned a trade at a very young age. Two years later, he studied with Francisco Pacheco, an influential artist who became his protector. At 18, he opened his own workshop and signed his first masterpiece, a work of amazing realism: *Old Woman Frying Eggs*.

Claude Monet (1840–1926)

He didn't like school, which he said "felt like a prison." Rules and discipline weren't for him! To keep from dying of boredom behind his desk, he amused himself by drawing his teachers. His portraits were so funny and brutal that, at age 15, his caricatures sold like hotcakes in his hometown of Le Havre. He made a bundle and was now convinced that he wouldn't be a businessman, like his father, but rather a painter.

Camille Claudel (1864–1943)

At an age when most little girls were playing with dolls, she preferred to sculpt clay. Determined, Camille had everyone under her thumb: She made her brother and sister help her find clay in the nearby forest and serve as models for her portraits. At age 12, she filled her home with clay busts. And at 17, she made her whole family move to Paris so that she could take sculpture classes. A true artist's temperament!

At a very young age, they dazzled those around them with their exceptional gifts. Here are the top 10 little Mozarts of the pencil, brush, chisel, or camera.

Pablo Picasso (1881–1973)

According to his mother, his first word was "piz," an abbreviation of "pencil" in Spanish. At age 6, Pablo could skillfully copy the artworks hanging in his home. At 8, he created his first painting and at 15, he was accepted to the Barcelona School of Fine Arts with *First Communion*, a painting that was already very mature. "It took me four years to paint like Raphael, but a lifetime to paint like a child," he later said.

Hergé (1907–1983)

In his childhood drawings, he already created stories in a series of panels, like a comic book. And his first heroes were teenagers with a "Boy Scout" personality, like himself but also like Tintin, whom he would come up with a few years later. He published his first comics in his middle-school newspaper and at age 17, he chose a new signature based on his initials, reversed. Georges Rémi became R.G. or "Hergé."

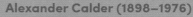

Alexander Calder (1898–1976)

The son of American artists, Alexander grew up around his mother's paintings and his father's sculptures. This stimulated his creativity. He made toys using a few bits of wood and pieces of string. He was a born tinkerer. Later, Calder kept up this interest and produced wire figurines and sculptures that danced in the air, his "mobiles."

Jean-Michel Basquiat (1960–1988)

He could read and write by age 4, and filled his school notebooks with sketches. His father threw him out of the house after he dropped out of school at age 17. He lived on the streets, sold sweatshirts and postcards that he painted himself, and covered the walls of New York City with graffiti. He drew with exuberant lines that overflowed with energy. His very distinctive style blossomed during his teenage years.

Henri Cartier-Bresson (1908–2004)

He grew up surrounded by art: His uncle was a painter, and he often went to the Louvre Museum to train his artist's eye. As a young man, he hesitated between painting and photography. Finally, he connected the two, by composing his photos like paintings and making photography into an art. He was even nicknamed "the eye of the century."

EXTRA-WIDE PAINTINGS!

A masterpiece isn't measured in feet and inches. But some artists were superheroes of painting, exerting their talent on canvases or panels that grew ever wider.

14.3 Feet
The Night Watch by Rembrandt, 1642
It took four years of work to paint this group portrait, which depicts a company of Dutch musketeers. This is Rembrandt's largest painting.

15.1 Feet
Screen with Cypress Trees by Kano Eitoku, late 16th century C.E.
Japanese warlords couldn't get enough of these splendid paintings on gold leaf. The cypress, a very hardy tree, is a symbol of strength in the Land of the Rising Sun.

32.2 Feet
The Wedding at Cana by Paolo Veronese, 1563
A painting of over 750 square feet, painted in only 15 months by one of the stars of the Renaissance in Venice!

16.3 Feet

The Death of Sardanapalus by Eugène Delacroix, 1827

Under siege in his palace, Sardanapalus, the legendary king of Assyria, chose to kill himself instead of surrendering. With this violent, turbulent painting, Delacroix showed great boldness.

26.6 Feet

The Abolition of Serfdom in Russia by Alfons Mucha, 1914

This painting is part of a cycle of 20 artworks tracing "The Slav Epic." It took the Czech painter almost 20 years to finish it.

205 Feet

The Electricity Fairy by Raoul Dufy, 1937

This is one of the largest paintings in the world. Dufy painted it in less than a year, just in time for the opening of the 1937 International Exposition in Paris!

72 Feet

Il Paradiso by Tintoretto (and his workshop), 1594

A gigantic paradise to decorate the Doge's Palace in Venice: this was the challenge that Tintoretto took up at age 70. The painting was completed by his workshop after his death.

THE CEILING OF THE SISTINE CHAPEL, A COLOSSAL TASK

It was a crazy idea: a gigantic illustrated Bible telling the story of the creation of the world, the first man (Adam) and the first woman (Eve), the story of Noah and the Flood, and much more. In only four years (1508–1512), Michelangelo achieved an artistic marvel. However, when Pope Julius II commissioned this painting for the Sistine Chapel in the Vatican, the artist was not at all excited about it.

The challenge seemed superhuman. Plus, he considered himself a sculptor, not a painter. But once he got started, nothing stopped him: not the dizzyingly high scaffolding where he had to twist his body or the backache that tormented him day and night. He even sent his assistants away and finished this colossal project alone, creating one of the most stunning masterpieces in the history of art.

The ceiling by the numbers
133 feet tall and **46** feet wide
66 feet above the ground
About **350** figures, including **60** in the Flood alone
9 scenes telling the biblical story of Genesis
12 figures of prophets and sibyls (ancient priestesses)
20 large male nudes
1 trompe-l'oeil architecture (having the illusion of depth)
to unite all these elements
4 years of "brute labor," according to Michelangelo
1 artist

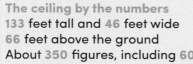
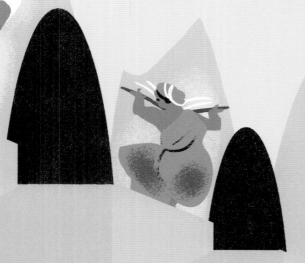

Notable quote:
Michelangelo had a hard time with the ceiling, which discouraged him and ruined his health. In one of his poems, he wrote that from "twisted work" he had his "belly beneath his chin" and his "beard turns up to heaven." As for the paint: "A rich embroidery bedews my face from brush drops thick and thin."

GOD IS GREAT, SO HIS MONUMENTS MUST BE TOO!

Temples, mosques, basilicas, or pyramids: everywhere, people have built signs of their faith. Here's a look at some massive sacred structures. Holy moly!

The Parthenon in Greece
Towering over the Acropolis of Athens, the Parthenon honors Athena, goddess of war and wisdom—and the city's protector. Despite the difficulties of transporting thousands of blocks of marble up to the top of the hill, the temple was built in record time, between 447 and 438 B.C.E. Greek sculptor Phidias decorated it with sculptures and a 524-foot-long frieze illustrating the Panathenaic Festival (dedicated to Athena). The nearly 40-foot-tall statue he built of Athena no longer exists. With this majestic monument, Athenians celebrated their city as much as they did their favorite goddess!

The Basilica of Our Lady of Peace in Côte d'Ivoire
The president of Côte d'Ivoire, also known as Ivory Coast, Félix Houphouët-Boigny had a dream: to build the biggest Christian basilica in the world in Yamoussoukro, in the middle of the African savannah. To make it come true, he launched this massive project. Completed in 1989 and nicknamed "the basilica of the Savannah," it holds several records: an extra-wide dome (295 feet in diameter), monumental colonnades, floors flowing with marble, and oversized stained-glass windows (the most stained glass in the world). The monument is even wider than its model, Saint Peter's Basilica in Rome.

The Great Mosque of Mecca in Saudi Arabia
At least once in their lives, all devout Muslims must go on the hajj, the "great pilgrimage" to Mecca. Its mosque holds the most holy sanctuary of Islam: the Kaaba, a small building shaped like a cube that contains a sacred black stone. Built between the 7th and 10th centuries C.E., the mosque has been expanded many times to accommodate the growing number of pilgrims. Today it is the largest mosque in the world and 900,000 of the faithful can gather within its walls. Its total area is over 4.3 million square feet, which equals 50 soccer fields!

Borobudur Temple in Indonesia
It is said to be the largest stone edifice in the Southern hemisphere, and the largest Buddhist monument in the world. For 1,200 years, its 1,600,000 stone blocks have looked out on the Indonesian jungle and the volcanoes of the island of Java. Seen from the sky, it looks like a mandala, a Buddhist representation of the universe. But from below, it is more like an enormous layer cake, with thousands of statues sticking up all over it. Visitors can walk along the passages and steps of this gigantic masterpiece for miles, ascending along the path of Buddha all the way to nirvana.

Pyramid of the Great Jaguar in Guatemala
Welcome to Tikal, an ancient Mayan city hidden deep in the jungle! It is a lost world, discovered in Guatemala in 1848. During its golden age between 200 and 900 C.E., the city had a population of over 50,000. Its Main Plaza still preserves the spectacular tiered pyramids built by the Mayans. One of the most impressive examples is 148 feet tall. The top holds a temple to the jaguar, a divine animal that was a symbol of power. Archaeologists also discovered the grave of a king under this temple.

THE GREATEST SCANDALS IN ART HISTORY

The Venus of Urbino by Titian, 1534
A completely naked woman on her bed, looking at the viewer self-confidently...this was unheard of in the 16th century! Until then, painters had been more discreet when depicting the goddess of beauty. For a long time, this painting was hidden from the public by another painting that covered it.

The Last Judgment by Michelangelo, 1541
When Michelangelo painted 400 figures without clothing on a chapel wall, and in the Vatican to boot, people certainly took notice! Horrified, Pope Paul IV had the private parts of Jesus and the saints covered up. Painter Daniele da Volterra was given this thankless task. After that, he was nicknamed Il Braghettone, or "the breeches-maker."

Death of the Virgin by Caravaggio, 1605
While artists had previously depicted the mother of Jesus rising to heaven surrounded by cherubs, Caravaggio produced a crude, realistic vision of her death. Her lifeless body lies there, arms hanging and feet dangling, like that of a mere mortal. Made for a church in Rome, the painting shocked the Italian monks, who refused to hang it. It went on to revolutionize religious art.

A Burial at Ornans by Gustave Courbet, 1850
A huge painting for an ordinary village burial.... unthinkable in the middle of the 19th century! Wealthier art patrons accused Gustave Courbet of a total lack of taste. But thanks to him, ordinary people— commoners and simple village folk—made their appearance in art.

The Nude Maja by Francisco de Goya, 1800
For a long time, in order to paint a nude woman, artists had to be sneaky and say that they were depicting goddesses.
Goya had had enough of this hypocrisy. His model was a real woman, in flesh and blood. She was curvaceous, with a mischievous look in her eye. The Inquisition, which controlled Spain with an iron fist, took Goya to court for obscenity. But this didn't stop his *Nude Maja* from fascinating generations of artists.

"We painters take the same liberties as poets and madmen,"
said the famous Italian painter Veronese.
Quite often, people have found these liberties shocking.
Here's proof with 10 mega-scandals.

Impression, Sunrise by Claude Monet, 1872
It's the port of Le Havre in the morning, painted with quick little brush strokes. Claude Monet tried to capture the sun's reflections on the water and the smoke from the ships. The painting sparked outrage, for it seemed blurry and botched. Monet was mockingly called an "impressionist," a term that ended up describing one of the most famous movements in painting.

Fountain by Marcel Duchamp, 1917
Can you make art without creating anything? Of course, Marcel Duchamp answered. He took a simple urinal, turned it onto its back, signed it, and gave it the title *Fountain*. Starting off as a prank, this "ready-made" shook up the way that people thought about art. From then on, what counted above all was the artist's approach, not what he or she created.

Woman with a Hat by Henri Matisse, 1905
A yellow and green face, garish colors from a tube that were applied directly to the canvas, broad brush strokes... Matisse was called crazy, savage, a "fauve" or "wild beast." And thus a new movement was born: Fauvism. Painters used colors with complete freedom, not caring if the result wasn't at all realistic.

Jeff Koons at the Château de Versailles, 2008
Known for his kitschy artworks, American artist Jeff Koons was invited to show 17 pieces in the most prestigious French venue: Versailles. This mixing of genres ruffled some feathers. Was his inflatable lobster meant to shock, or was it a nod to the Sun King's extravagance and excess? One thing is sure: the scandal created a lot of buzz, and further increased the artist's popularity.

Monument to Balzac by Auguste Rodin, 1898
Auguste Rodin was tasked with creating a monument in honor of the writer. The result was puzzling: only Balzac's head emerged from a large coat. "He's a snowman!" "It's Balzac in a hospital gown!" the critics mocked. They didn't understand that with this powerful silhouette, reduced to the essential, Rodin had pushed sculpture into modernity.

SERIAL PAINTERS

These series of artworks depicted the same landscape dozens of times. It's a duel between Monet, the Impressionist master, and Hokusai, the champion draftsman.

Claude Monet (1840—1926)

During his life, the Impressionist star often painted 20, 30, or even 100 versions of the same subject, seen from the same angle. These series were designed as sets. This was something new in Europe! But, before him, in Asia, another artist was a pro in this area: Japanese artist Katsushika Hokusai. Since his teenage years, Monet had collected prints by Hokusai, precious engravings on paper.

Why was he crazy about series?

Because Monet noticed one day that the landscape he had started painting in the morning had changed in the afternoon. It seemed blue at sunrise, yellow in the sunlight, and then pink in the light of dusk. To capture these changes, he worked on several paintings at the same time, moving from one to another according to the time of day.

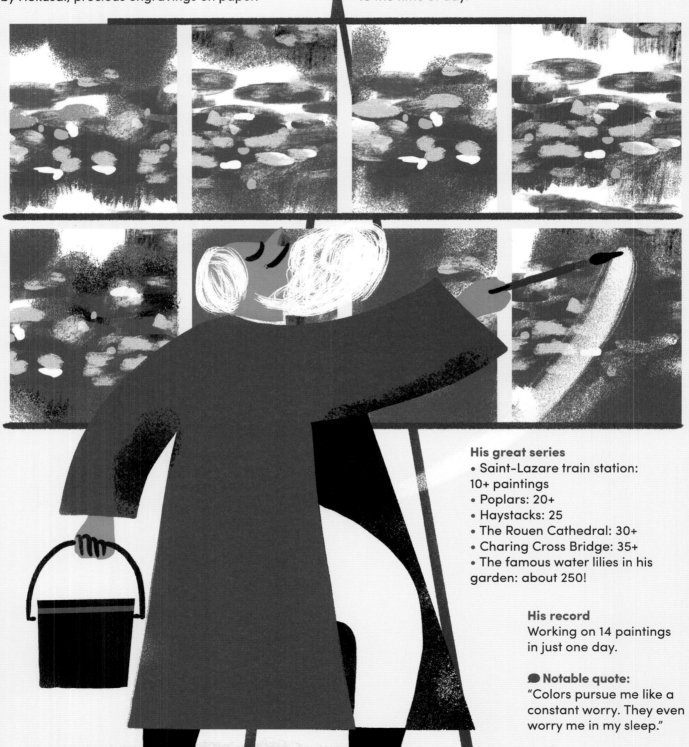

His great series
- Saint-Lazare train station: 10+ paintings
- Poplars: 20+
- Haystacks: 25
- The Rouen Cathedral: 30+
- Charing Cross Bridge: 35+
- The famous water lilies in his garden: about 250!

His record
Working on 14 paintings in just one day.

💬 **Notable quote:**
"Colors pursue me like a constant worry. They even worry me in my sleep."

Hokusai (1760–1849)
Over his 70-year career, he made thousands of paintings, drawings, prints, and illustrated books. He was truly a "Gakyō Rōjin," someone who is "mad about painting," a nickname he gave himself in later life. His prints became very famous in 19th-century Europe and influenced Monet and van Gogh.

Why was he mad about series?
To show the beauty of the Japanese landscape, he roamed across the country with his sketchbooks in his pocket. Mount Fuji, the sacred mountain of Japan, fascinated him. He depicted it up close, from afar, at dawn and at dusk, in good weather, struck by lightning, in mist, and in the snow.

His record
He is said to have made 30,000 drawings during his lifetime.

Notable quote:
"All I have done before the age of 70 is not worth bothering with." He has a point, because he made his greatest masterpiece, *Thirty-Six Views of Mount Fuji* (1831), at age 71!

His great series
Mount Fuji: 146 prints. *The Great Wave* is the most famous one from this set.

CHAMPIONS OF THE SELF-PORTRAIT

5+
Albrecht Dürer
(1471—1528)

In the Middle Ages, painters were considered craftspeople and rarely signed their paintings. Painting a self-portrait would have seemed quite pretentious. That changed in the Renaissance, which emphasized art and the individual. We see this with Dürer, the first "fine gentleman" of painting. He didn't hesitate to use himself as the sole subject of his painting. And he painted himself as a gentleman, or even as Jesus Christ. He was also the first to paint himself nude.

💬 "When I was led to a table, the people moved to either side, as if a fine gentleman were passing by. Among them there were also prominent figures who all bowed deeply, showing me the greatest respect."

15 +
Gustave Courbet
(1819—1877)

He was handsome, and he knew it. He had the face of a Romantic hero, and he trusted himself most of all to immortalize it many times over. "Mr. Courbet has a very handsome face that he loves to reproduce," writer Théophile Gautier mocked. In fact, the painter did more than that. He revealed his state of mind at various times of his life: with the confidence of youth, happy and in love, or in the throes of desperation.

💬 "I'm the proudest and most arrogant man in France."

40+
Vincent van Gogh
(1853—1890)

How can you learn to design and paint portraits if you can't afford to pay a model? By looking in the mirror! That's what van Gogh did. In just a few years, between 1885 and 1890, he produced around 40 self-portraits, in which he tried to capture his features truthfully. Sad, worried, or distraught, his eyes reflected the torments that consumed him.

💬 "I purposefully bought a mirror good enough to enable me to work from my own image in default of a model, because if I can manage to paint the coloring of my own head... then I could also paint the heads of other good souls, men and women."

Painting one's own portrait is a longstanding tradition for artists.
But what about painting dozens of them? Were these obsessive self-portraitists
just big-headed? It's not that simple.

50+
Frida Kahlo
(1907—1954)

Out of her 143 paintings, around 50 are self-portraits. She expressed her personality, Mexican roots, and very personal pain, such as the bus accident that destroyed her body, her difficult love story with Diego Rivera, and her inability to have children. With Frida, the self-portrait became a way to overcome trauma.

💬 "I paint myself because I'm so often alone, and because I am the subject I know best."

80+
Pablo Picasso
(1881—1973)

From age 15 all the way to 91, he never stopped sketching his own face, and each time in a different style. Through his self-portraits, we can follow all the major periods of his art: academicism, his blue and rose periods, Cubism, a return to Classicism, Surrealism, and more—the list is long!

💬 "In painting, we can try everything. We even have the right to. As long as we never repeat ourselves."

100+
Rembrandt
(1606—1669)

The Dutch artist depicted himself at every age. With the regularity of a metronome, for 40 years, he painted, engraved, or drew his reflection: the young man with wild hair, the painter who was proud of his success, or the old, lonely man. With an increasingly free technique, he marked the passage of time.

💬 "When I want to ease my mind, it isn't honor that I seek, but freedom."

THE CRAZY PALACE OF POSTMAN CHEVAL

Art can appear where we least expect it. It can even be made by men and women who have never studied painting, sculpture, or architecture. Led by their dreams and driven by an exceptional will, they can move mountains. Like Ferdinand Cheval (1836–1924), a postman in Hauterives, a village in the department of the Drôme in France. Every day, even in wind and rain, he walked over 18 miles through the countryside to deliver the mail. And to help pass the time, he traveled in his head. He dreamed about the places on the postcards filling his sack: Hindu temples, mosques, chalets, and more.

He began to imagine his own "ideal palace." And then one day—April 19, 1879—his foot struck a stone with an unusual shape. "Since Nature provides sculptures, I will be an architect and mason," he decided. He had never held a trowel in his life, but he was not discouraged, stuffing his pockets with stones for his building. At night, he would take more stones to his garden with his wheelbarrow. People thought he was crazy. But when his work was finally complete, 33 years later in 1912, they were amazed. And today, his palace is one of the most beloved monuments in France.

Notable quote:
"I sought and I found
For forty years I shoveled and dug
To make this fairy palace rise up out of the earth
For my idea, my body braved it all
Weather, the critics, the years
Life is a swift courier
My thoughts will live on in this stone"

The "Ideal Palace"
by the numbers
85 feet long
46 feet wide
39 feet tall
33 years of constant work
10,000 days (and nights) of labor
1 architect, mason, and sculptor:
Postman Cheval
1 "faithful companion:"
his wheelbarrow

THE VERY FIRST...

Starting in 1850, the Industrial Revolution transformed the world with its scientific and technical advances.
Art also started a revolution, and became modern!

1850—1857
First art photography
The landscapes of Gustave Le Gray
Photography was invented in 1826 by Nicéphore Niépce.
Less than 30 years later, it became an art.

1886
First pointillist painting
An Afternoon on the Island of La Grande Jatte **by George Seurat**
When he decided not to mix colors, but instead to place
little dots of color side by side, this 26-year-old artist paved the way
for the explosive hues of Matisse and the Fauves.

1907
First Cubist painting
Les Demoiselles d'Avignon **by Pablo Picasso**
Picasso was 26 when he painted these five
women, whose angular lines were inspired by
African sculpture. Modern art was born!

1910
First abstract painting
Untitled **by Wassily Kandinsky**
Kandinsky in Germany, Malevich in Russia, Mondrian in Holland,
Kupka and Delaunay in Paris: At almost the exact same time, in
different countries in Europe, artists took a grand leap into
abstraction. Their paintings no longer represented a clearly
identified subject, but colorful shapes.

1912
First collage
Fruit Dish and Glass **by Georges Braque**
Mixing pieces of wallpaper with drawings
may seem very normal today, but around a
century ago it was revolutionary!

1918
First monochrome painting
White on White **by Kazimir Malevich**
A completely white painting produces a
sensation of infinite space. Malevich was the
first to try this radical experiment.

1947
First drip painting
Cathedral by **Jackson Pollock**
With a brush or a long stick, Pollock splashed and dripped paint onto the
canvas. Art became gestural: this was called "action painting."

1963
First video art
13 Distorted TV Sets **by Nam June Paik**
As television entered people's homes, two
artists had the idea of using it as an artistic
medium: South Korean artist Nam June Paik
and his friend, German artist Wolf Vostell.
This was the birth of video art.

1956
First Pop composition
Just what is it that makes today's homes so different,
so appealing? **by Richard Hamilton**
It's considered a founding work of Pop Art, which is
"popular, transient, expendable, low-cost, mass-produced...
sexy, gimmicky, glamorous, and Big Business," according
to British artist Hamilton.

HEAVYWEIGHTS OF CONTEMPORARY ART

Bernar Venet

Born in southern France in 1941, he got noticed for coating his canvases in a layer of tar. He continued his experiments in New York, and in the early 1980s became excited about straight or curved lines. They can be found in his monumental sculptures, which have made him known throughout the world.

His record

Arc Majeur: an arc of a circle that bursts from either side of a highway in Belgium. Reaching 197 feet high and completed in 2019, this sculpture is the largest in Europe. It took 6,500 hours of welding and assembly to put together its 200 tons of steel.

His favorite material

Corten steel, which is very durable, with a rusty appearance (also Richard Serra's favorite!).

How does he do it?

He first works with shapes using aluminum wire and makes a model. Then production happens in a factory. Once they are smelted, the steel bars are transported in massive trucks and put together using cranes. Engineers check the quality of the soil, because the sculptures need to stay firmly anchored! At the Château de Versailles, where Bernar Venet was invited to exhibit his work in 2011, he removed some of the paving stones from the Place d'Armes and dug with excavators to anchor two arcs that were 72 feet long.

American artist Richard Serra and French artist Bernar Venet are truly sculptors of the impossible. Let's look at these two magicians of steel.

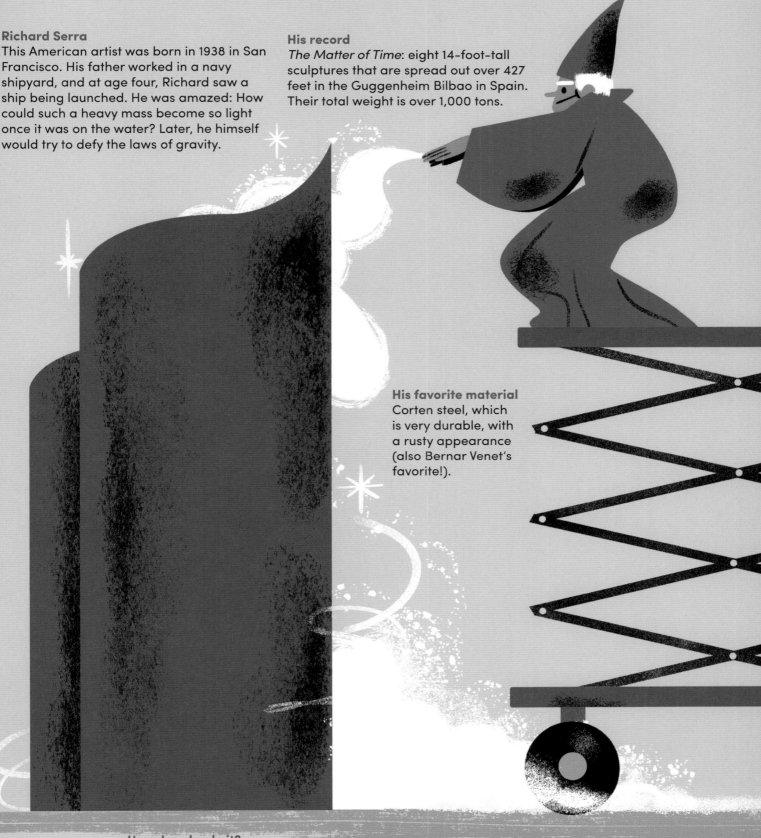

Richard Serra

This American artist was born in 1938 in San Francisco. His father worked in a navy shipyard, and at age four, Richard saw a ship being launched. He was amazed: How could such a heavy mass become so light once it was on the water? Later, he himself would try to defy the laws of gravity.

His record

The Matter of Time: eight 14-foot-tall sculptures that are spread out over 427 feet in the Guggenheim Bilbao in Spain. Their total weight is over 1,000 tons.

His favorite material

Corten steel, which is very durable, with a rusty appearance (also Bernar Venet's favorite!).

How does he do it?

Richard Serra starts with a model. Then he builds his sculpture using a computer program that calculates the positon and angles of the plates. The artworks are made in a factory. Then, another project begins: installation. The plates are so heavy that before they are placed in a museum, its floor must be reinforced. Then they are lifted by cranes and positioned at an angle calculated down to the millimeter, which guarantees their balance. It's an extremely precise process.

HIGHER AND HIGHER...

Starting in the late 19th century, new construction techniques pushed the limits of architecture. The whole world became crazy about reaching new heights! The race for the highest tower hasn't stopped yet.

1,483 feet
The Petronas Towers in Kuala Lumpur
These two towers can't be missed. Their endless spires rise in the capital of Malaysia and contain the offices of the oil company Petronas. At night, they shine like two laser beams. The numbers are staggering: each 88 stories tall, with 32,000 windows in all. It takes three months to clean all the windowpanes! When they were completed in 1998, the towers were 33 feet taller than the Sears Tower in Chicago, one of the tallest American skyscrapers. Asia was about to outdo America.

1,250 feet
The Empire State Building in New York
In the early 20th century, New York grew a forest of skyscrapers. These buildings were elegant and dizzyingly high, like the Empire State Building, which thrust itself toward the sky over more than 100 stories. How was it possible? By using a frame of steel that supports the entire building. The walls are only a casing and can be opened with thousands of windows. This symbolic monument of American modernity, completed in 1931, was the tallest building in the world for 50 years.

1,063 feet
The Eiffel Tower in Paris
Lighter and more durable than stone, iron could do amazing things, as Gustave Eiffel was well aware. With this material, he built bridges, viaducts, and the framework of the Statue of Liberty. So why not the tallest tower in the world? To meet this challenge, the engineer imagined it as an assembly kit: the 18,038 pieces of the Eiffel Tower were manufactured and partly assembled in a factory. They just had to be put together like a piece of furniture on the Champ-de-Mars. In 1889, 7,300 tons of iron rose into the air to a height that had never been seen before.

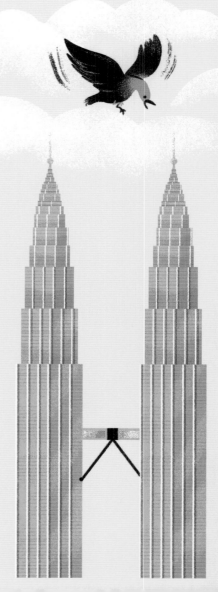

1,667 feet
The Taipei 101 in Taipei

This turquoise "bamboo shoot" completely dominates the other skyscrapers that surround it. It has 101 stories (hence its name) and the fastest elevators in the world. They propel visitors up to the 89th floor in just 37 seconds! The structure, made of high-performance steel, is designed to withstand earthquakes and typhoons, which are common in this part of Southeast Asia. To make it even more stable, a 660-ton ball of steel was placed internally near its peak.

1,815 feet
The CN Tower in Toronto

A landmark of the Toronto skyline since 1976, the CN Tower is a gigantic antenna for the city's television and radio reception. It's also a very popular tourist attraction. Workers had to dig 49 feet deep and remove 56 tons of earth to anchor this concrete arrow and its seven-story sphere, which contains a rotating restaurant and two panoramic viewpoints. Daring visitors can hang above the void attached to a harness.

2,717 feet
The Burj Khalifa in Dubai

This is the tallest building in the world (for now)! With this 163-story "rocket" that opened in 2009, the small Arab Emirate of Dubai showed its power and its technology. The builders were able to conquer the sandy soil, propel the concrete ever higher, and transport materials using massive cranes. This mega-project involved 12,000 workers who put up one story every three days, in sometimes-terrible conditions. The next challenge: to go beyond the symbolic limit of 1 kilometer, or .6 miles, tall.

THE MOST EXPENSIVE PAINTINGS IN THE WORLD

Has the art market gone crazy? Collectors are fighting over artworks and spending millions in the process. Here are some of the most expensive paintings in the world.

$450,000,000
Salvator Mundi, attributed to Leonardo da Vinci, around 1500
This Christ as "savior of the world" is the most expensive artwork ever. It was purchased by the kingdom of Saudi Arabia. However, according to some experts, this painting is not by Leonardo da Vinci but one of his pupils.

$300,000,000
Interchange by Willem de Kooning, 1955
A high score for Willem de Kooning. In the 1950s, with other American artists (such as Jackson Pollock), he invented a new way of painting that was very gestural and colorful: Abstract Expressionism.

$210,000,000
When Will You Marry? by Paul Gauguin, 1892
During his lifetime, Gauguin had a lot of trouble selling his splendid Tahitian paintings. Today they sell for skyrocketing prices. This image of two young Tahitian women was bought by the small but ultra-wealthy kingdom of Qatar. It was subsequently resold to an undisclosed buyer.

$250,000,000
The Card Players by Paul Cézanne, 1895
Two men confront each other face to face...a real duel, but with cards! The royal family of Qatar paid an astronomical sum for this masterpiece by Cézanne, one of the fathers of modern art. There are four other versions of these players, all held by museums.

$200,000,000
Number 17A by Jackson Pollock, 1948
After World War II, Pollock gave a big boost to American art by smacking and dripping his brushes onto huge canvases. His inventiveness and his early death, at only 44 years old, made him a legend.

$186,000,000
No. 6 (Violet, Green and Red)
by Mark Rothko, 1951
Like Jackson Pollock, Rothko was a major painter of 1950s America. His paintings took the shape of large colorful areas that engulf the viewer like a soothing balm.

$179,000,000
The Women of Algiers by Pablo Picasso, 1955
Picasso is ever more popular. The price for this painting, a tribute to the painter Delacroix and his *Women of Algiers* (1834, Louvre Museum), soared beyond $150,000,000 in 11 minutes of bidding!

$170,000,000
Reclining Nude by Amedeo Modigliani, 1917
When it was shown in Paris in 1917, this very sensual nude painting caused a scandal, and the police demanded it be taken down. Almost 100 years later, the painting once again caused a frenzy, this time among buyers.

$165,000,000
Masterpiece by Roy Lichtenstein, 1962
"Why, Brad darling, this painting is a masterpiece!" murmurs the woman in this painting. Message received by collectors, who are crazy about American artist Roy Lichtenstein's Pop Art style, inspired by 1950s comics.

$135,000,000
Portrait of Adèle Bloch-Bauer by Gustav Klimt, 1907
In the club of the most expensive artists in the world, we also find Austrian artist Gustav Klimt, who is famous for his decorative paintings combining painted figures and gleaming adornment. In this painting, Adèle Bloch-Bauer, the wife of a rich manufacturer, is set in an ocean of gold.

TRAFFIC JAM AT THE MUSEUM

With massively expanding tourism, museum attendance has exploded.
All over the world, people rush to see famous artworks, and, most of all, to immortalize the experience. Selfies are everywhere, and the lines get longer and longer.
Here are the top five most-visited museums in the world.

National Museum of China, Beijing
Expanded in 2010, it is now the second-largest museum in the world (the Louvre is first). This colossal building, whose white façade looks out on Tiananmen Square, is devoted to Chinese history and culture. More than 8.5 million people visited it in 2018. Porcelain, coins, and ancient bronze statues are there alongside paintings to the glory of Mao and the People's Republic of China.

Louvre Museum, Paris
This former royal palace is in first place, with over 10 million visitors in 2018. The majority are from the U.S. or China, and they want to see the Mona Lisa above all. To get a selfie with their idol, they're willing to brave the crowds, the lines, and the jostling, forgetting that the museum features many other remarkable women: the *Venus de Milo*, *The Penitent Magdalen* (Georges de La Tour), *Madame Récamier* (David), the *Grande Odalisque* (Ingres), and many more.

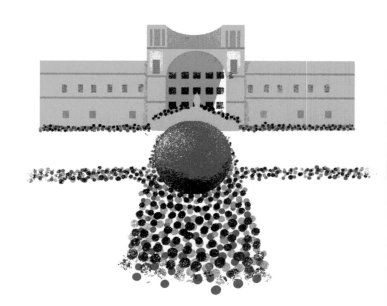

Metropolitan Museum of Art, New York City
The Metropolitan, also known as The Met, was founded 150 years ago. Some 2,000 people work there overseeing its encyclopedic collections: Greek and Egyptian antiquities, armor, costumes, arts of Africa and Asia, paintings and drawings by masters such as Michelangelo, Caravaggio, Poussin, Vermeer, van Gogh, Hopper, and many more. Increasing numbers of people flock to see it: there were over 7 million of them in 2018!

Vatican Museums, Rome
The museums of the papal city are overflowing with masterpieces: the sculpture group *Laocoon*, the *Saint Jerome* by Leonardo da Vinci, the Raphael Rooms, and, of course, the Sistine Chapel. In 2018, over 6.7 million people walked under the ceiling painted by Michelangelo! This causes traffic problems: Once visitors finally get into the chapel, they are quickly pushed toward the exit. A more serious concern is that the heat, dust, and humidity produced by the crowds endanger the frescoes.

Aiuto! Venice is flooded by tourists.

Crowds rushing to see a historic city, a museum, or a monument? Usually, this is good news. As long as this enthusiasm doesn't threaten the places being visited. Venice has become the symbol of uncontrollable tourism, with 30 million visitors per year. Every day, thousands of tourists pour from 10-story cruise ships into the small Italian city, which cannot absorb so much traffic. The result: Saint Mark's Square is packed, public transportation is overloaded, no one can get through the narrow streets, souvenir shops are everywhere. Venice is starting to become "Veniceland," and its residents have had enough and are leaving. Even more concerning, the huge cruise ships are causing waves that damage the wooden pilings that support the city. If Venice can't stem the tide of mass tourism, the most beautiful city in the world could end up sinking.

JR'S LIMITLESS ART

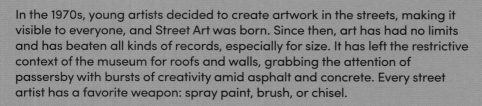

In the 1970s, young artists decided to create artwork in the streets, making it visible to everyone, and Street Art was born. Since then, art has had no limits and has beaten all kinds of records, especially for size. It has left the restrictive context of the museum for roofs and walls, grabbing the attention of passersby with bursts of creativity amid asphalt and concrete. Every street artist has a favorite weapon: spray paint, brush, or chisel.

French artist JR (born in 1983) always has his camera and tub of glue on hand. He takes photos of anonymous people, unrecognized heroes of the everyday, and sticks giant images of their faces onto the walls of their city. In 2008, he went to a *favela*, or slum, in Rio de Janeiro, Brazil, where drugs and violence were rampant. JR took photos of the women who lived there despite the danger and then stuck their giant portraits to the façades of houses. It was a way of giving a different appearance to the city.

The project *Women Are Heroes* by the numbers
1 camera
20 portraits of women
stuck to **20** houses in the Morro da Providência *favela*
for **20** days
with help from **4** Brazilian steeplejacks
over a total area of almost **14,000** square feet

Notable quote: "It's a randomly assembled project, like the *favela* itself. We managed to do it despite the sloping streets, rickety houses, unpredictable electric lines, and the gunshots that sometimes struck several houses."

THE ULTIMATE RECORD-HOLDERS!

Ciao! It's me, the Mona Lisa.
No one can beat me when it comes
to world records.
I'm the painting that's...

The most speculated about
They've said it all. For instance, that I was a self-portrait of Leonardo da Vinci, a man disguised as a woman. The truth is much simpler! I'm the portrait of a lady from Florence, Lisa del Giocondo. And since "gioconda" means "happy" in Italian, I'm smiling.

The most protected
Six guards, surveillance cameras, a safety barrier, reinforced glass...the French government makes a big deal about my safety!

The most famous
In 1911, a thief removed me from the wall and took me to Italy. The whole world was upset about my disappearance! Two years later, they found me safe and sound and brought me back to the Louvre. But no more peace and quiet! I had become a global star.

The most adventurous
Leonardo took me with him to Milan, Rome, and then France. After he died, I spent time at the Châteaux of Fontainebleau and Versailles and then ended up in the Louvre. And what about more recently?
In 1962, I took a ship to the U.S. (first class, of course!). And in 1974, I headed for Japan, where people love me, and then went on to Moscow. But ever since, I haven't gone anywhere. They say I'm too fragile and I can't travel anymore.

The most photographed
Every day, 20,000 people wait in line and jostle each other to get a photo of me and take a selfie. Multiplied by 365, that means 7 million admirers per year. Keep moving!

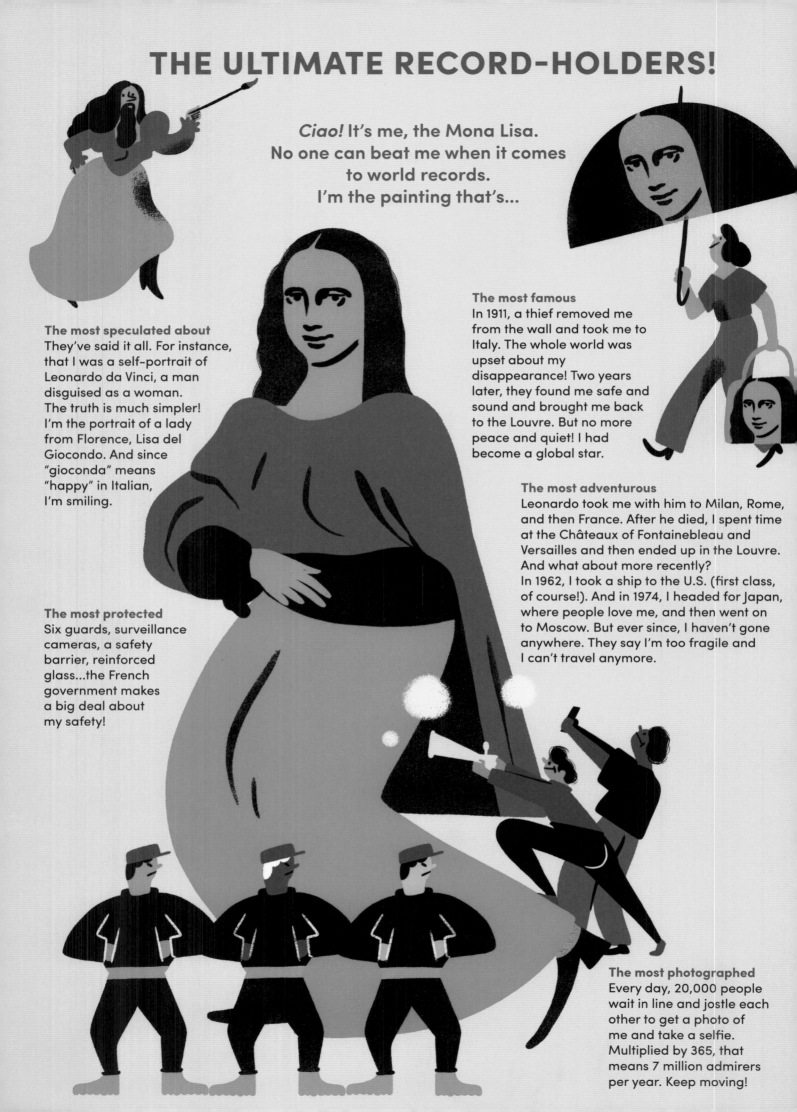

Hola! I don't need to introduce myself — everybody knows who I am. I'm Picasso, a genius, a giant, a myth! I'm the artist who is...

The most productive
I'm a hard worker and I can make a drawing in a flash. Since the age of 8, I've never stopped: I've made over 60,000 artworks during my lifetime, which means an average of more than two a day.

The highest-priced
During my lifetime, my art already sold for higher prices than anyone else's. Today, I make buyers go bonkers, and they'll spend tens or even hundreds of millions for my paintings!

The most legendary
My artworks are super-famous, and my life is, too. All the great photographers want to take my picture, and all the museums want to show my work. After my death, Picassomania reached new heights. In 2011, I was the star of 69 exhibitions!

The most inventive
Modern art owes everything to me. Cubism, this chaotic style that breaks forms into a thousand pieces, that's ME! The invention of the collage and relief paintings, ALSO ME! Using recycled items to make art (bike seat + handlebars = bull's head), ME AGAIN! I constantly experiment and create a new style whenever I feel like it.

Amazing Artworks: The World's Biggest, Oldest, Most Jaw-Dropping Creations
first published in the United States in 2022 by Tra Publishing
Text by Éva Bensard © 2021, Éditions Arola
Illustrations by Charlotte Molas © 2021, Éditions Arola
Edited by Antoine Ullmann with Laetitia Le Moine and Christian Nobial
Graphic design by Studio Fouinzanardi
Translated by Kate Deimling and reviewed by David Auerbach
for Eriksen Translations, Inc.
Original title: *Le grand livre des records de l'art*

Printed and bound in China
ISBN: 978-1-7347618-9-4

Amazing Artworks is printed on Forest Stewardship Council
certified paper from well-managed forests.
Tra Publishing is committed to sustainability
in its materials and practices.

FSC
www.fsc.org

MIX
Paper from
responsible sources
FSC® C102842

Tra Publishing
245 NE 37th Street
Miami, FL 33137
trapublishing.com

T tra.publishing

The illustrations in this book were created in the style of works by artists both
ancient and modern. The following works are protected by copyright:

Raoul Dufy
La Fée Électricité (The Electricity Fairy), 1937
© 2021 Artists Rights Society (ARS), New York / ADAGP, Paris

Bernar Venet
L'Arc majeur, 2019
© 2021 Artists Rights Society (ARS), New York / ADAGP, Paris

Richard Serra
The Matter of Time, 1994–2005
© 2021 Richard Serra / Artists Rights Society (ARS), New York

JR
Women are Heroes, 2008–2009
© JR